JULIA CUNNINGHAM

The Stable Rat

and Other Christmas Poems

PICTURES BY
ANITA LOBEL

GREENWILLOW BOOKS
An Imprint of HarperCollinsPublishers

With love to all the children,
and to Susan Hirschman, then and now
—J. C.

To the memory of Christmas with
the Lillys
—A. L.

Julia Cunningham

The Stable Rat and Other Christmas Poems
Text copyright © 2001 by Julia Cunningham
Illustrations copyright © 2001 by Anita Lobel
All rights reserved. Printed in Singapore
by Tien Wah Press.
www.harperchildrens.com

Watercolor paints and a black pen were
used to prepare the full-color art.
The text type is Seagull.

Library of Congress Cataloging-in-Publication Data

The stable rat, and other Christmas poems / by Julia
Cunningham ; illustrated by Anita Lobel.
     p.   cm.
"Greenwillow Books."
ISBN 0-688-17799-9 (trade).
ISBN 0-688-17800-6 (lib. bdg.)
1. Christmas—Juvenile poetry. 2. Animals—Juvenile poetry.
3. Children's poetry, American. [1. Christmas—Poetry.
2. Animals—Poetry. 3. American poetry.]
I. Lobel, Anita, ill. II. Title.   PS3553.U477 S72 2001
811'.54—dc21   00-048440

1 2 3 4 5 6 7 8 9 10 First Edition

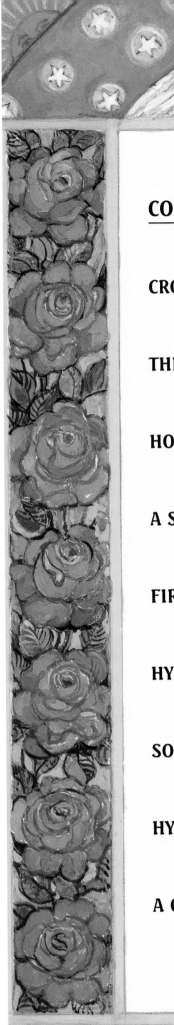

CONTENTS

CROWS ON A CERTAIN EVENING

What a gathering it was,
a choir of caws,
voices all giving out
with hoarse Hosannas,
and when the foxes mocked them
they went right on
into mighty hymns
that thundered the tops of trees,
tossing their leaves
every which way.
A triumphal blast of trumpets
in the days of Rome
would have been a whisper
beside what came out
of those beaks,
and all because their reason
for rejoicing was born
under one of their stars.

THE STABLE RAT

- 1 -

I am a shadow, gray, gray, gray—
  never lightened by scarlet or splotched gold
 or even a dot of the green I see
 when I gaze from the cracks,
  peering out of my necessary night.
 I have often wondered,
  what if I swallowed a tiny lantern?
 Would my black eyes brighten
 and show me where to go
 other than here in this hostel
 of beam and board and rafter?
 I've heard the others, know their shapes
 as clearly as my own:
  the donkey braying at the foolishness of hens,
 the cow content to give her daily pail of milk,
 never withholding her placidity,
  the horse too old for harnessing, who wakes to eat,
  the sheep, clotting their corner
  in four mounds of wool
   white as moons.
   They hear my teeth gnawing to keep them sharp,
   they see my tail over the edge of sacks,
   my mouth feasted full of grain,
   but never turn to look, to recognize.
   I beg their attention and in my pain
   shriek like the prongs of pitchfork against stone.
   I am alone and gray, forgotten,
    a fill of skin so small among their legs.
    They stare where I am not,
     no thing to name,
      no presence to be known.

That was then, but when this evening came
two strangers entered here,
two-legged, and the one wrapped round in cloth
lay down in straw, the other hovered over,
and soon the two were three.
I crept warily to where she lay
as did the others move close and closer still,
breathing upon the one
who had been born beneath this roof.
The donkey shunted me away with thrust of hoof,
the horse loomed, and the hens
hopped so near, their feathers stirred his hair.
The sheep became a wall to block the wind
that seeped from every stall,
and I was left outside the circling of him.
Then I saw his hand grope for the shadow
that was me.
His fingers clutched my tail
and lovingly he turned me round to see.

Suddenly I became green and gold and scarlet,
haloed by a flame, a fire as was he,
a rising higher than the evening star—
a glory given me,
shadow and self together.

HOW DID THE ANIMALS KNOW?

How did they know, what told them standing there
roofed under rough-hewn beam and rotted rafter?
What quieted the ox and caused the mare
to whinny twice, a hen to cluck like laughter?
Why did three shepherds usher in six sheep
to form a wall of warmth across the door?
How did they know that child so deep asleep
upon the straw of this hoof-hardened floor
would wake a world? Was it a winged spirit
entering their silences who came
speaking in hums that they might better hear it,
a heralding of Him, this child without a name?
Grunt and crow, squeal and bark and bray,
they raised hosannas to this blessed day.

A SHEEP SPEAKS

I stand within my wool and wonder.
There's been a great scurry ever since the sky blued
and the wind stilled.
Our leader looked up, pointing his nose at a star,
and the rest of us, as we always do,
looked up and pointed too.
Why?
I am puzzled.
Our shepherd begins to sing croakily
and nobody seems to care that he stutters the words.
Even they are strange like the snatch I caught—
"Alleluia"—whatever that means,
it's certainly not sheep talk.
Three shining people mounted on long-necked beasts,
cloaked in purple with gold circles on their heads,
are heading for our stable.
I wish I could follow them
but I've learned never to stray,
just pretend
when I want to leave the flock.
 So I stand here within my wool
  and send my other self,
   trot, trot, trot,
    to where something, someone waits
     to solve my wonder.

FIRST LIGHT

When the Great Star gave way to sun,
such a wakening burst into the morning,
even the sheep forgot to eat grass.
The barnyard cock danced with the rat,
and a passing gull who could not sing
sang a hymn. The three kings
spoke quick poems in their languages
no one understood, but their joy was recognized
and the shepherds no longer felt
a necessity to bow. Instead they formed
a choir and shouted rhymes
they had learned as children.

All this time the mother smiled
and, gazing at what she saw was beautiful
in her child, remembered what the angel
had told her and quite suddenly became a queen
although she never wore a crown.

HYMN

A little mouse
was born that night
beside a stranger
full of light
who shared his manger
as his house.
Sing low, sing high,
both he and I
together lie.
So shall all meet.
Sing true, sing sweet!

SONG FOR THE CHILD

The still, small breathing of this child
cored a whirlwind. There a mild,
soft stir of straw and moving sheep
awoke a century from sleep.
A lantern swung an arc of light
across the weeping face of night,
and to a world that gave no home
the many-mansioned child had come.

HYMN TO JOY

Give greatly of your grunts, O pig!
Scratch deeply of your joy, O hen!
Sing out in choired squeaks, O mouse!
To herald in the boy. Amen.

The tiger's head shall know His hand
and bow that He may stroke his ears,
the lion lend his ropey tail,
the jackal joke away His tears.

The donkey will receive His weight,
a tree will grow into His cross,
a new horizon birth such light
as burns and blazes out the loss.

So bray your best, O simple ass!
Release your cheeps, O little wren!
Trumpet down stars, O elephant!
Announce our love! Amen.

A CHILD'S SONG FOR A CHILD

Be my flower,
Be my star.
Lend me a breath
Of what you are.

Partaking of the rose
I might
Candle myself
A little light.

Or journeying
Within your space,
Be fragranced by
A little grace.

Be my morning,
Be my day,
All my hours,
Greened or gray.

Be my borning,
Risen up.
Be my vaulted
Midnight cup.

Be whatever mystery
You are—
Like me mysterious—
But be!

Julia Cunningham made history in 1965 with
the publication of her groundbreaking book <u>Dorp Dead!</u>
Among her many honors are the Christopher Medal
for <u>Come to the Edge</u> and a Boston Globe-Horn Book Honor
for <u>The Flight of the Sparrow</u>. Her <u>The Treasure Is the Rose</u>
was a National Book Award Finalist.
Julia Cunningham lives in Santa Barbara, California.

Anita Lobel received a Caldecott Honor for <u>On Market Street</u>.
Her books have been chosen by the <u>New York Times</u> as among
the year's best illustrated three times and have received countless
other awards. Among her most popular books are <u>A Rose in
My Garden</u>; <u>One Lighthouse, One Moon</u>; and <u>Alison's Zinnia</u>.
Her account of her wartime childhood in Europe,
<u>No Pretty Pictures</u>, was a National Book Award Finalist.
Anita Lobel lives in New York City.